Shaping Your
Career

Pocket Mentor Series

The *Pocket Mentor* Series offers immediate solutions to common challenges managers face on the job every day. Each book in the series is packed with handy tools, self-tests, and real-life examples to help you identify your strengths and weaknesses and hone critical skills. Whether you're at your desk, in a meeting, or on the road, these portable guides enable you to tackle the daily demands of your work with greater speed, savvy, and effectiveness.

Books in the series:

Leading Teams
Running Meetings
Managing Time
Managing Projects
Coaching People
Giving Feedback
Leading People
Negotiating Outcomes
Writing for Business
Giving Presentations
Understanding Finance
Dismissing an Employee
Creating a Business Plan
Managing Stress
Delegating Work
Shaping Your Career

Shaping Your Career

Expert Solutions to Everyday Challenges

Harvard Business Press

Boston, Massachusetts

Library of Congress Cataloging-in-Publication Data
Shaping your career : expert solutions to everyday challenges.
       p. cm. — (Pocket mentor series)
    "James Waldroop and Timothy Butler, mentors"—P. .
    Includes bibliographical references.
    ISBN 978-1-4221-1876-4
    1. Career development. 2. Career changes. 3. Vocational qualifications.
4. Vocational interests. 5. Self-management (Psychology)—Problems, exercises, etc.
I. Waldroop, James. II. Butler, Timothy. III. Harvard Business School Publishing
Corporation.
    HF5381.S5145 2008
    650.1—dc22

                                                        2007037466

The paper used in this publication meets the requirements of the American National Standard for Permanence of Paper for Publications and Documents in Libraries and Archives Z39.48-1992.

Contents

Knowing Yourself   15

Ideas for identifying the business activities that engage you most.

Clarifying who you are   16

Looking inward   16

Asking others   17

Using formal assessment tools   19

Knowing when it's time for a change   20

Understanding Business Interests   21

Ways to recognize the activities you most enjoy on the job.

Eight core interests   22

Figuring out your core interests   24

Clarifying Your Work Reward Values   27

Strategies for articulating the rewards you want to get from your job.

What are work reward values?   28

Why clarify your work reward values?   29

Strategies for clarifying your work reward values   31

Assessing Your Skills   35

Ways to take stock of your on-the-job abilities.

Understanding types of skills   36

Knowing your strongest skills   37

Tips and Tools   57

Mentors' Message: Why Take Charge of Your Career?

A company thinks strategically about its positioning in its industry and the value of its products and services. This strategic focus helps it remain competitive and profitable. Likewise, you need to think about your position within your organization and the value of your skills and interests.

Organizations large and small now realize that, in order to remain competitive in a fast-changing world, they need employees who regularly assess their work interests, values, and skills. By constantly clarifying what you want to learn next and then taking the steps to obtain that knowledge, you become increasingly valuable to your company. You also stand an excellent chance of finding renewed satisfaction in your work.

But keep in mind: Your career is not a one-time decision made early in life. Rather, it's an iterative process that you refine and redefine as you grow professionally. In this guide, you'll find a wealth of suggestions and strategies for managing that process. All of this takes time and some extensive inquiry into who you are and what kinds of work you find most stimulating. But the effort will pay big dividends: By continually shaping your career, you boost your chances of deriving immense satisfaction from your work as well as making your best possible contribution to your organization.

James Waldroop and Timothy Butler, Mentors

Drs. James Waldroop and Timothy Butler are business career psychologists who worked together for almost twenty years at the Harvard Business School. Dr. Butler is now Senior Fellow and Director of Career Development at the Harvard Business School. They have spent many years helping businesspeople work through the career planning and development processes. Their online business career assessment tool, CareerLeader, is used by more than 400 universities and corporations around the world. (For more information, go to www.careerleader.com.)

They are also the authors of four highly acclaimed *Harvard Business Review* articles as well as three books: *Getting Unstuck: How Dead Ends Become New Paths*, *Maximum Success: Changing the Twelve Behavior Patterns That Keep You from Getting Ahead*, and *Discovering Your Career in Business*. They are frequent contributors to the national media, with articles in *Fortune* and *Fast Company*, and have appeared on radio and TV to discuss issues related to managing your career, retaining talent, and maximizing personal effectiveness.

Shaping Your Career: The Basics

What Does Shaping Your Career Mean?

T HE PROCESS OF assessing where you are in your work life, deciding where you want to be, and then making the changes necessary to get there is called *shaping your career*. It's an ongoing process that *you* orchestrate and that you must manage, thanks to important changes in the business arena.

Understanding the need for change

The world is changing fast, including the world of work. The increasing pace of change that has marked recent decades can leave you breathless sometimes, whether you're a manager in a large corporation, an entrepreneur running your own business, an individual contributor in a small company, or an independent contractor providing services to clients.

When it comes to your career, change is natural—and it's healthy! You strengthen your professional abilities every time you take on new challenges, gain insight into what you want from your work, and learn a new set of skills. You then find more satisfaction in your work *and* contribute more to your organization.

Growing at your company

As you think about redefining your career path (or discovering a new one), take care that you don't fall victim to the all-too-common migration temptation—the belief that if you're unhappy in your job, you should go to another company. The fact is that it may not be your *company* that's the problem. More likely, it's something about your current *role*.

You stand an excellent chance of finding renewed satisfaction in your work if you take advantage of opportunities at your company that match best with your interests, by either enhancing your current role or taking on one or more entirely new roles within the firm. Your company benefits, too, because it now has an even more loyal employee (you!), without incurring the costs of evaluating, hiring, and training someone to replace you.

Organizations large and small now realize that, in order to remain competitive in a fast-changing world, they need employees who:

- Are dedicated to the idea of continuous learning

- Regularly assess their interests, values, and skills so as to figure out the kinds of work for which they are best suited

- Are committed to their company's success

- Understand the skills and behaviors the company will need in the future—and are willing and able to respond quickly and flexibly to develop those capabilities

- Can move easily across functional boundaries and between regular duties and special projects

What Would YOU Do?

Old Dog, New Tricks?

DAVID HAD AN epiphany: He didn't want to work in advertising anymore. He liked the people, but he was realizing that he no longer found his career stimulating. Then reality set in. He thought to himself: "I'm too old to start from scratch. Too old to learn new skills. And too old to go back to school."

Yet David realized that he had years of valuable knowledge and experience. Everyone said he was a great manager, and he had a knack for understanding client needs.

Then it hit him. "I'm *not* too old to start something new—I'm too young to give up on my dreams!" But where should he start? What should he do to start moving himself in the right direction?

What would YOU do? The mentors will suggest a solution in *What You COULD Do.*

Navigating the job-change process

Even though change is natural and healthy, that doesn't mean it's always easy. Managing your own professional development entails some focused effort on your part. First (and most critical), you have to know yourself. Knowing yourself means that you can articulate how the following categories apply to you.

- Your most passionate *business interests* are the kinds of work you're most passionate about.

- Your deepest *work values* are the rewards—such as autonomy, money, close working relationships with colleagues—that you consider most important.

- Your strongest *skills* are your abilities, the things you have learned how to do, such as use a spreadsheet program for data analysis.

Second, you need to become familiar with the many different development opportunities and resources your company has to offer. And third, you pursue those opportunities that you've identified are best for you.

This process can be both exciting and daunting. Prepare to feel stuck at times and to feel that things are moving way too fast at other times. The good news is that many resources are available to help you through the career growth process—including support and insight from your colleagues, friends, and family. You can also take advantage of a selection of formal assessment tools to help you clarify your interests, values, and skills.

If you know what to expect ahead of time, you'll be better able to navigate the change process.

What You COULD Do.

Remember David's desire for change in his career in advertising?

Here's what the mentors suggest:

As David begins the process of thinking about a new career, he might ask himself the following questions:

- What are his core business interests—that is, what types of work is he most passionate about? For example, does he prefer problem solving, working with people, or making decisions?
- What are his deepest work values? For example, does he care more about having autonomy or earning a big salary?
- What are his strongest skills?

Once he has identified the answers to these questions, he will be on his way to defining and navigating a new career path or a new direction within the career he's currently in.

Taking Charge
of Your Career

IN TODAY'S BUSINESS environment, the "contract" between employer and employee no longer exists in many companies. So it's up to you to continually define and direct your own career.

Defining your career

The idea that employees should be in charge of their own professional development is relatively new. In the past, people expected to choose a career early in life, find an employer, and then stay at that company for the rest of their working lives. The company was the plane, its leaders were the pilots, and the employees were the passengers. Today, everyone is a pilot.

In the past, in return for their loyalty and longevity at the company, employees received all sorts of protections—including job security, a steady rise up the corporate ladder (with corresponding increases in income), and a retirement pension.

Today, that "contract" between employer and employee no longer exists in many companies. Why? A confluence of radical changes has rewritten the rules of the workplace. These changes include technological advances, globalization, a boom in entrepreneurship and a proliferation of new, small, fast-moving companies, and a wave of reengineering and restructuring that has led to flatter and leaner organizations.

Such changes mean that the skills required for any company to stay competitive—whether large or small, new or mature—keep shifting at an ever-increasing rate of speed.

Shifting your skills to stay competitive

Today, workers must update and broaden their abilities more frequently and use a wider variety of skills—whether they're employees of a company or entrepreneurs running their own businesses, or whether it's early or late in their professional lives. Middle managers especially have felt the impact of organizational flattening. For instance, managers' responsibilities and roles have shifted so dramatically that many people are no longer sure how to define the term *manager*! And due to layoffs and restructurings in recent decades, many managers have lost their jobs or have had their responsibilities redefined in not-so-desirable ways.

These scenarios can pose difficulties for even the toughest among us. However, there's also a bright side to the picture: As companies reinvent themselves, new opportunities for growth emerge that no one would have dreamed of a few years ago.

You can play a proactive part in these changing times. How? By taking charge of your own career development— that is, by constantly clarifying what you want to do next and learn next and then taking the steps necessary to find those opportunities and obtain that knowledge.

Also, professional development doesn't necessarily mean changing your career or job or discovering your ideal career for the first time, as a person new to the workforce would do. It can also mean growing and increasing your satisfaction *within* your current role and professional path. This is far healthier—and more stimulating—than getting caught in a job rut doing the same thing year after year. And it makes you a far more valuable employee to your company.

Thinking career lattice, not ladder

In today's work world, career development is for *everyone*—no matter what your industry, position, or age. To grasp the differences between today's and yesterday's employment "rules," compare career-ladder thinking with career-lattice thinking, as shown in the table "Examples of career-ladder and career-lattice thinking."

Examples of career-ladder and career-lattice thinking

Career-ladder thinking	Career-lattice thinking
I move up or down the corporate ladder.	I can move up or down *or* side to side.
My boss has all the answers.	My colleagues and I must figure things out.
The longer I stay at the company, the more rewards I'll receive.	The more I improve my learning, contributions, and performance, the more rewards I'll receive.
My company is responsible for its own success.	I and each of my colleagues are responsible for our organization's success.

Thinking strategically about your career

Your company is constantly thinking strategically about its positioning in the industry and the value of its products and services. Likewise, *you* can constantly think strategically about your place in the company and the value of your work interests and skills.

By regularly attending to your development and updating your skills, you become increasingly valuable to your company. You can also derive more and more satisfaction and stimulation from your work.

What if you work for a small company or have launched your own business? You can still think strategically about your career. And you'll probably feel even more responsible for your professional growth. Why? Because, unlike many employees in large corporations, you won't have access to an in-house career center or company-sponsored professional development programs—leaving your career development entirely up to you.

Knowing
Yourself

T HE MOST IMPORTANT step in managing your career is getting to know yourself. This is true whether you're just beginning your career, established in one but wishing you could change in some way, or happy where you are but still wanting to improve certain aspects of it.

Clarifying who you are

Knowing yourself includes articulating things such as what types of work you like to do, what kinds of environments you prefer to work in, what sorts of people you like to work with, what abilities you possess, and what abilities you need to develop. In other words, to define and navigate your career path, you need to identify your most passionate core business interests, your deepest work values, and your strongest skills.

How do you go about identifying these? You have three sources of information: looking inward, asking others, and using formal assessment tools.

Looking inward

To use yourself as an information source, look deep within yourself to identify key themes. You can do this by using checklists or worksheets that help you clarify your core interests, values, and skills. You can also engage in some short mental exercises to get to know yourself better. Here are just a few.

- **Articulate what makes you unique.** Ask yourself what you cherish most about yourself. What is most special about you? What are your unique gifts?

- **Look for imagery.** Leaf through some magazines and find a picture that you think best represents who you are. Ask yourself why you chose that particular image.

- **Envision your entire life.** Imagine that you are at the end of your life, looking back over your entire work history. Finish these sentences: "I am most proud of _____." "I wish I had done more of _____."

Notice what the results of these activities suggest about your interests, values, and skills.

Asking others

The people who know you best often become excellent sources of information about your work interests, values, and abilities. Indeed, if you imagine yourself as the CEO of your own professional growth, you can think of these people as your board of directors.

Try these activities to build self-knowledge with the help of your personal board.

- **Consult your colleagues.** If you work in a large or small organization, ask colleagues, "What's my reputation in the company? What am I best known for?"

- **Interview your friends.** Pick five or six people who know you well. Ask them questions such as these: "What four words would you use to describe me?" "If your best friend asked you to tell her more about me, what would you say?" "What do you see as my driving force? What makes me tick?"

- **Ask people who know you well to write letters to you—anonymously (to get their most honest feedback).** Invite several people to write a letter to you, about you. (Tip: Choose a mix of people, for example, a colleague, a supervisor, a family member, a college friend, a social friend, your partner, and even an adult son or daughter.)

Provide your board members with a form that lists the following questions and includes spaces where they can write or type their answers. Ask them to use the third person ("Pat enjoys . . .") in their responses.

- "What would be the ideal work for me?"

- "What seems to make me most fulfilled and excited?"

- "What work should I stay away from, and why?"

- "What about myself do I have trouble seeing?"

- "What aspects of myself do I need to change to be more successful?"

- "What aspects of myself should I not change?"

Collect all the responses and look for common themes. These themes will provide clues to your interests, values, and skills. Be sure to thank your board members for their honesty and thoughtful attention. They'll appreciate knowing that you're using the information and insight they've provided.

Using formal assessment tools

A broad array of formal assessment tools can help you clarify your deepest interests, values, and skills. For some of these, you might want to see a career counselor, who will administer the tests and interpret them for you. For others, you can take the tests and interpret the results yourself. CareerLeader, a career management tool created by the mentors, is an online assessment tool you can use on your own as well as with the help of a career counselor.

Tip: To pick the right career counselor for you, ask potential candidates—whether internal or independent— to describe their philosophy, explain what kinds of clients and questions they typically work with, and describe their successes and the methods they used to achieve them. If you're a successful executive or manager, look for someone with a lot of experience helping people at your level. Be leery of counselors who use the same approach with everyone. This can indicate poor training and limited ability. In career counseling, one size *doesn't* fit all.

If your company's human resources department has a career counselor who uses assessment tools, pay a visit and see if you can schedule a time to take any tests you're interested in. If that option isn't available, consider hiring a career counselor to help you with the tests.

Knowing when it's time for a change

There's another important part of knowing yourself: recognizing when it's time to explore new work opportunities. The signals can differ for each person. The table "Are you ready for a change?" can help you determine whether you've outgrown your current role and would relish new experiences. Check "Yes" or "No" for each statement.

Are you ready for a change?

I am experiencing . . .	Yes	No
A feeling of dread when Monday morning rolls around		
Envy of what others are doing for work		
Restlessness		
Boredom		
A recurring sense of repetition in my work		
A growing interest in nonwork areas of my life, such as a course I'm taking or a home-improvement project I'm considering		
Inability to see a future that I want to move toward		
A tendency to overreact to small problems		
A need for more intellectual challenge, financial compensation, autonomy, or another major work reward value		

Interpreting your score: If you checked "Yes" for most of these statements, you are probably ready for a change in your professional life.

Understanding
Business Interests

YOUR CORE BUSINESS interests—the activities that you most enjoy doing—are the most important elements to understand about yourself when you're considering reshaping your career. By gaining familiarity the full range of possible core business interests, you can begin determining which ones you might have.

Eight core interests

Through extensive research, we have identified eight core business interests that people can have. Your core interests remain relatively stable over your lifetime, so they're an excellent foundation on which to base your career. We've organized the eight interests into the following three categories. The first category, *Application of Expertise*, includes these interests:

- **Application of Technology:** getting involved in the inner workings of things; being curious about better ways to use technology to solve business problems; feeling comfortable with mathematics, computer programming, and physical models of reality
- **Quantitative Analysis:** engaging in problem solving that relies on mathematical analysis—frequently, but not always, financial analysis
- **Theory Development and Conceptual Thinking:** taking broadly conceptual approaches to problem solving; having interest

in and comfort with abstract ideas, imagination, theory, plans, scenarios, and forecasts

- **Creative Production:** taking part in highly creative activities, ones in which you bring something new into being— whether that something is a creative product as such or a new way to make sealing wax

The second category, *Working with People*, consists of the following interests:

- **Counseling and Mentoring:** helping others to grow and developing relationships as an integral part of business work
- **Managing People and Relationships:** dealing with people and interpersonal issues daily

And the third category, *Control and Influence*, is made up of these interests:

- **Enterprise Control:** having ultimate decision-making authority for an enterprise, division, or project: the power to set the strategy and to ensure that the strategy is carried out
- **Influence through Language and Ideas:** persuading others through the skilled use of written and spoken language (whether you're talking to one person, a small group, or a large audience)

Figuring out your core interests

Most people have between one and three core business interests, some of which may be stronger than others. For example, you may be fascinated by quantitative puzzles and feel great satisfaction in helping other people learn to solve problems as well. Your core interests may manifest themselves differently at different times. For example, if your interests are Creative Production and Application of Technology, perhaps in childhood you loved writing stories and plays. Then, in your teenage years, you enjoyed devising mechanical gadgets. Later, as an adult, you desired a career in design engineering or movie production.

You can identify your core business interests by learning what typical activities express the various interests and then seeing which of those activities you find most appealing. The table "A closer look at core business interests" gives examples of such activities.

A closer look at core business interests

CATEGORY 1: APPLICATION OF EXPERTISE

Application of Technology	Quantitative Analysis
Examples:	*Examples:*
• Engineering	• Analyzing cash flows and investments
• Programming computers	• Analyzing market research
• Planning production tasks and systems	• Forecasting
• Designing product and processes	• Building computer models
• Analyzing processes	• Creating production schedules
• Analyzing systems	• Performing accounting tasks
• Crafting and manufacturing	
• Researching	

Theory Development and Conceptual Thinking	Creative Production
Examples:	*Examples:*
• Developing economic theories	• Designing new products
• Developing business models	• Marketing and advertising

- Analyzing the competition
- Designing "big-picture" strategies
- Designing processes
- Teaching business theory

- Generating new ideas
- Developing innovative approaches and solutions
- Being an entrepreneur
- Managing projects
- Conducting public relations

CATEGORY 2: WORKING WITH PEOPLE

Counseling and Mentoring

Managing People and Relationships

Examples:

- Coaching, training, teaching
- Performing organizational development
- Managing human resources
- Fostering mentoring-oriented management
- Supporting and developing people
- Providing feedback and advice

Examples:

- Managing others to accomplish the goals of the business
- Directing
- Supervising
- Leading others
- Motivating
- Taking care of day-to-day operations

CATEGORY 3: CONTROL AND INFLUENCE

Enterprise Control

Influence through Language and Ideas

Examples:

- Controlling resources to actualize a business vision
- Setting the strategic direction for a company, business unit, work team, or division
- Having ultimate decision-making authority
- Making deals
- Holding ultimate responsibility for business transactions, such as trades, sales, and so on

Examples:

- Negotiating
- Deal-making
- Conducting public relations
- Selling
- Persuading
- Designing advertising campaigns
- Communicating ideas through writing or speaking

To determine your core interests, you could also try these exercises.

- Think about times when you've been so absorbed in what you were doing that you lost track of time—whether what you were doing was work related or not. (Psychologists call this the experience of *flow*.) Then try to understand what really pulled you into that flow and how that might translate into something you do at work.
- Think about whether you're envious of any particular colleagues. That is, do they have jobs that you wish *you* had? Ask yourself what activities these people perform that you wish you could do. Then, recall previous jobs you've held. Ask yourself what kinds of activities you kept gravitating toward.
- Remember times when you've been working on projects. Which *stages* of a project excite you the most—the planning stage? Implementation? Follow-up?

What do the answers to all these questions suggest about your core business interests?

Finally, consider using assessment tools or other self-reflection exercises and activities that can help you gain insights about yourself.

Clarifying Your Work Reward Values

W HILE IT'S VITAL to understand your core business interests in shaping your career, your work values are also important.

What are work reward values?

People mean many different things when they speak of values. For example, many of us speak of family values, national values, or spiritual values. But *work reward values* constitute a special set of values. Specifically, they're the values you place on the various rewards that you might get in return for performing your job. They refer to the rewards that motivate you to do any parts of your work that you're not intrinsically interested in—the dessert you get for eating the things you may like a little less well.

Here are some examples of work reward values.

- **Financial rewards** include financial security and stability. They might take the form of a predictable salary, specific types of benefits, future employment, and the opportunity to acquire wealth.

- **Task rewards** include intellectual challenge and variety.

- **People rewards** are associated with affiliation—the opportunity to work with colleagues you like and admire. They might also include getting recognition from your superiors.

- **Career rewards** provide you with access to people and opportunities that will position you well for your next career move.

- **Lifestyle rewards** such as work/life balance allow you time to pursue other important aspects of your life, such as family or leisure activities.

Why clarify your work reward values?

Clarifying your values offers several benefits. For one thing, it increases the likelihood that you'll choose satisfying work. It may be difficult to find one position that satisfies all of your desires. But if what you're doing for work doesn't provide *enough* of the rewards that you consider most important, you probably won't remain happy in it for very long.

Moreover, clarifying your values lets you shop more efficiently for the right developmental opportunities. Just as you can evaluate a potential computer purchase much more quickly if you keep a few must-have features in mind, you can judge a work opportunity more wisely if you remember your most crucial rewards.

Finally, clarifying your values helps you match them to the culture of an organization or a department. Work rewards manifest themselves in a workplace's culture—the way people do things, what they expect, what they think is most important, and so forth. A large company's different departments (for example, engineering, sales, or human resources) might have *markedly* different cultures. By knowing your values, you can pick the culture that will provide those rewards.

What Would YOU Do?

Getting to Know Me, Getting to Know All about Me

CARLY HAS BEEN manager of new business development for ZyMold for five years. One evening after a long day, she got together with Tonya, a friend who had recently changed jobs. Carly found herself feeling envious as Tonya excitedly described her new position. Carly mentioned that she recently received a raise and retention bonus, but she just wasn't as enthusiastic about her work as she once was. She told Tonya that although she likes her team, she senses that something's missing from her work life.

Tonya replied, "It sounds like you need to take a close look at how you feel about your job. Maybe the work just isn't a good fit for you anymore." Carly agreed. But later that night, she found herself wondering exactly what to do next to reshape her career. Should she organize a couple of informational interviews? Talk with someone in HR about job openings elsewhere in the company? Where should she begin?

What would YOU do? The mentors will suggest a solution in *What You COULD Do.*

Strategies for clarifying your work reward values

Most people are pretty clear on what work rewards motivate them most strongly. But if you need help clarifying your work reward values, one way is to use checklists or worksheets such as the ones provided in the Tips and Tools section of this book.

Another strategy is to analyze experiences you've had in the work world. For example, suppose you've held a position where the rewards you got for the work (perhaps job security or task variety) just didn't matter to you. In this case, ask yourself what would have motivated you more in that role.

Or recall a time when you interviewed for a job, and the interviewer was talking at length about a reward that you just didn't care about. But when he switched gears to a different reward, you found yourself far more interested. This response to discussion of more appealing rewards can clue you in further to your work reward values.

NOTE: In clarifying work reward values, many people face a common temptation to list values they think they *should* have—such as altruism—and to avoid listing values they think they *shouldn't* have—such as desire for prestige or financial gain. Be as honest as you possibly can when articulating your values. Genuine answers will make it much easier for you to evaluate and choose the best possible work opportunities for you.

Steps for Clarifying Your Work Reward Values

1. Write all the work rewards you can think of on index cards, one reward per card.

2. On each card, write a short statement about what that reward means to you. For example, your idea of work/life balance might be working no more than forty hours a week.

3. Scatter the index cards on a table.

4. Arrange the cards in order of importance. If two or more rewards seem equally important to you, place them side by side. If you decide that a reward has no real importance to you after all, set that card aside.

5. Note the order you've settled on. Don't worry about whether you're having trouble deciding which of two seemingly equally important rewards should come first. Just draw a picture that summarizes what you see happening at this stage.

6. Set the stack of cards aside for a week or two.

7. Revisit the exercise to see if anything has shifted.

8. Think of your top three or four rewards as your shopping list when you're considering new developmental opportunities.

What You COULD Do.

Remember Carly's concern about what to do next to begin reshaping her career?

Here's what the mentors suggest:

Carly should start by assessing how well her current role fits her core business interests and reward values. She can begin by compiling a record of her thoughts and feelings about her work responsibilities and environment. This record should consist of a private, running list of what she likes and doesn't like about her job or work environment. The entries could be about her own role as well as other people's work and about tasks, relationships, or the work environment itself. Entries might range from simple ("I need to work near a window") to more complex ("I can't stand working alone for long periods of time").

Honesty is key in creating such a record. Carly should see what themes and patterns emerge in the entries. And she needs to consider what these themes tell her about her core business interests and reward values. For example, perhaps the entries in her list suggest that she is most stimulated by helping others or applying technology to business problems. And perhaps they indicate that she feels happiest in a role that offers a collaborative work environment, job security, or intellectual challenge.

continued

By gaining insight into her core business interests and reward values, Carly will be well on her way to generating ideas for re-shaping her current role so that it's more satisfying or for moving to a new role at ZyMold or elsewhere.

Assessing
Your Skills

I N ADDITION TO clarifying your core business interests and work reward values, it's helpful to assess your skills—the abilities you possess and those you may want to develop in order to excel in a given role. To assess your skills, start by gaining familiarity with the types of skills generally found in the workplace.

Understanding types of skills

As you progress through your work life, you acquire many different skills from a broad range of experiences and training. Skills fall into a number of categories, and there are different ways to describe them. The table "Skill categories" shows some examples.

Skill categories

Category	Examples
Communication	Making presentations, writing marketing copy, interviewing job candidates
Technology	Working with spreadsheets, using graphics or presentation software, designing circuit boards
Finance	Creating a budget, assessing costs, preparing business plans
Supervision	Hiring employees, delegating tasks, assessing people's performance
Management	Managing projects, leading a change initiative, solving business problems

Knowing your strongest skills

As you begin exploring developmental opportunities at your organization, you'll need to know which skills they require. That way, you can decide to what extent these opportunities will allow you to do one or more of the following:

- Use skills you already have in abundance

- Stretch skills that you possess to some degree but would like to strengthen

- Obtain entirely new skills

The first step, though, is to take stock of your existing skills and to assess which ones are your strongest. There are several ways to do this. For example, you can experiment with assessment tools, checklists, and short exercises (like the ones presented in the Tips and Tools section). You can ask your friends, family, and colleagues to give their opinions about what you do best. And you can consult a career counselor.

Articulating your transferable skills

When assessing your skills, it's especially important to identify your transferable skills. These are skills that have value regardless of the business context in which you're using them. Transferable skills include writing, motivating others, organizing data, and interpreting information.

Why is it important to know your transferable skills? Knowing this information allows you to widen the selection of potentially interesting work opportunities to include all those in which you would use your transferable skills. It also helps you avoid the common misconception that, in order to try a new work area, you need to develop a whole new set of skills. You may realize you *don't* necessarily need to go back to school to develop new skills for a different opportunity. When you know your skills, you can market yourself to potential new supervisors in a whole new area of work by pointing out your transferable skills.

TRANSFERABLE SKILLS *n* Abilities that have value regardless of the business context in which they are being used.

Four key points about skills

In assessing your skills, keep these points in mind.

- **Skills are a threshold variable in your ability to do a job successfully.** You need *enough* of a certain skill (being able to lift 50-pound bags, for example), but in many cases, having a lot more of that same skill (being able to lift *500*-pound bags) won't make you any *more* successful.

- **Skills are much less stable than interests or work reward values.** That is, you can strengthen existing skills or acquire new ones through practice, training, and new experiences. And you can let skills deteriorate if you no longer use them on a regular basis.

- It's perfectly okay to have both strengths and weaknesses. Often, when people begin exploring new positions at work, they assume that they have to be good at just about everything. The fact is, we all have both strengths and weaknesses—that's part of what makes us who we are. Don't feel bad if you lack certain skills; everyone does.

- You need to weigh the benefits of developing new skills. Investing in skill development can be costly, in terms of time, effort, and money (possibly). So, when you're evaluating a potential new opportunity at work, spend some time deciding whether you want to invest in developing the skills that the opportunity requires.

Steps for Defining and Obtaining New Skills

1. Identify what you need to learn and why you need to learn it. Consider a variety of skill types—including functional, transferable skills (such as clear writing or working with numbers), task-oriented skills (for example, writing a computer program in a particular language or assembling a particular consumer product), personal skills (including being organized or juggling many tasks at once), interpersonal skills (such as the ability to lead a discussion or negotiate), and industry-specific skills (those required for performance of a particular job).

2. Select the ways you might be able to learn. Cast your net wide! You've got many different options for learning at your

disposal—in addition to the more commonly known ones such as going back to school. Also, different people learn best through different learning channels and materials. Then think about which channels and materials work best for you—home-study courses, direct observation of someone else, internships, volunteer work, films, workshops, and online learning programs are all good possibilities.

3. Conduct research to identify specific learning options. Explore resources such as professional associations, career centers, adult-education centers, university extension offices, and the Internet.

4. Analyze your learning options, weighing matters such as quality of instruction, cost, time required, and location.

5. Develop a training strategy and schedule. Clarify how and by when you'll acquire the skills.

Finding Developmental Opportunities at Your Company

ONCE YOU'VE ASSESSED your skills, the next step is to get a complete picture of who you are by combining the skills information with what you learned about your core business interests and work values. You can now use this knowledge and information to redefine your current role. You can also begin evaluating the growth opportunities available at your company and pick the most appropriate ones for you.

Throughout this process of gaining knowledge and information about yourself and your interests, values, and skills, remember: Interests and values matter the most. When evaluating a career development opportunity, make sure that it matches your *core business interests* and *work values*. If it does, you may well decide to obtain the skills that will help you perform in that new position.

Starting the search

You've worked to identify your deepest business interests, clarify your most important work reward values, and assess your strongest skills. Maybe you've even defined a career opportunity target. What's the next step on the path? Many companies have an explicit process in place to enable employees to explore and pursue new opportunities. For example, your organization might suggest that you visit its career management center, review the job bank, and then follow the guidelines.

Other companies ask that you first talk with your supervisor. That way, he or she can become aware of your search and help you either redefine your current role or identify potential opportunities elsewhere in the organization.

Indeed, in most organizations, helping direct reports clarify their goals and find appropriate growth opportunities are important responsibilities for managers. By supporting you in this way, your manager helps the organization retain a valued employee—a key step for any company that wants to stay competitive in today's economy. You can provide the same kind of support for your direct reports.

There are many ways to identify potential growth opportunities throughout your company. The key is to make sure you *know your company*.

- In simplest terms, what work does the organization do?

- What are your company's biggest needs and challenges?

- How do you think you could contribute to your company's efforts in ways that suit your deepest interests, values, and skills?

Finding out what people do

You also need to find out what kinds of work people do throughout the organization. Knowing this will give you a big picture of how the company functions. Of course, gathering all this information takes some research and a willingness to get to know people who can help you. Here are some ideas to get you started.

First, *use your company's career management resources.* Many companies offer numerous ways to learn about growth opportunities. Find out what they are—and take advantage of them. These include:

- Career centers staffed by career counselors and research specialists

- Internal networks of people who are willing to talk with any fellow employee about their jobs

- Opportunities to sample different jobs by filling in for colleagues who are on sabbatical

- Job banks describing all the positions available in the organization

- Reference materials and training to help you create a professional growth plan and hone your résumé-writing and interviewing skills

- In-house courses on various subjects and skills related to jobs within the company

- Tuition reimbursement programs for college or vocational school

Second, *build your network.* Networking simply means getting to know people in your organization who can help you learn about and pursue career opportunities. To become an expert networker, ask yourself: "Who knows the most about what's going on in the organization?" Then seek out opportunities to meet those people and talk with them about your search.

> **Tip:** In your company directory, identify people who do work that interests you, and get to know them. Tell them you're clarifying your professional development goals, and ask to have a conversation with them sometime about their work.

Third, *cultivate relationships with mentors*—experts from whom you can learn, in detail, about specific kinds of work and strategies for defining a career path. Mentors can be people who work in your organization or outside your organization, members of professional associations—anyone whose experience and knowledge you respect.

> **Tip:** Establish mentoring relationships with (1) one person within your company (your company mentor), (2) another person who has mastered the area of expertise you're interested in (your skill mentor), and (3) someone whose overall career path you find enviable (your career strategy mentor). If possible, at least one mentor should be someone outside your company.

And fourth, *consult a career counselor*. Many organizations have career counselors on staff who can advise you on how to spot potential development opportunities. If your organization provides this service, make an appointment. If not, consider having a couple of sessions with an independent career counselor. These professionals' services can be pricey, so be sure to shop around for the best choice for you. On the other hand, someone who charges more but can help you better and faster may ultimately be a bargain for you.

Choosing the right growth opportunities

When making decisions about which growth opportunities to pursue, ask yourself questions such as these: "How good is the fit between the position and my interests, values, and skills?" "How good is the fit between the position and who I want to become?" (That is, "What kinds of *learning opportunities* does this position offer me?") The best developmental assignments are ones in which the fit is imperfect—the position will stretch you by offering challenges that encourage you to learn new skills and acquire new knowledge.

Of course, stretch positions carry some risk. You won't be able to make your most productive contribution right away. After all, you'll need time to learn the new dimensions of the job. The challenge is to pick an opportunity that doesn't stretch you *too* much or carry *too* great a risk. As a general rule of thumb, the risk is probably too great if it seems that you'll need more than six months to learn enough to make a meaningful contribution.

Getting the skills you need

There are lots of ways to enhance your skills, including on-site training, adult-education courses, distance learning, and online courses. One key thing to remember, though, is that you *don't* always need to go back to school to make a major change in your career. Before you commit to spending a lot of money (and time) on a new degree, do some research to make sure there isn't a more affordable and less time-consuming way to master the skills that your new position requires.

Getting the information you need

Once you've identified possible development opportunities, it's time to arrange some informational interviews. You can conduct

Steps for Preparing for an Informational Interview

1. Think of three to five individuals who are currently doing the kind of work you're interested in.
2. Contact them (by phone, by e-mail, or in person).
3. Set a time and meeting place for an appointment.
4. Prepare a list of questions you'd like to ask the interviewee.

these interviews with people who are currently doing the kind of work you're interested in, with supervisors, or with department or division heads who can give you valuable information about the work.

Informational interviewing is less formal than actual job interviewing because it gives you a chance to learn more about positions of interest and helps you get to know potential new supervisors and other people in departments or divisions of interest. It also lets you showcase your talents and may give you further insight into additional interesting positions. (Even if an interview reveals that a particular new job wouldn't work out for you, you can use the encounter as another networking opportunity by asking the interviewee to suggest more people for you to talk with.)

The key to setting up informational interviews is to be sincere and honest when contacting potential interviewees. If you're nervous about contacting people, remember that you're asking for information, not a job offer. Also, most people are happy to talk about their work, if you respect their time (ask for no more than twenty minutes) and clearly value the information they offer. Finally, people are especially open to meeting with you if you've been referred to them by someone they know and respect. So, broach the subject of an interview by saying something like, "Hello, my name is _____. I'm currently working as a _____ and am interested in learning about _____. My colleague _____ mentioned that you'd be a great person for me to talk with. Could I have twenty minutes of your time when it's most convenient for you?"

Steps for Defining Your Career Target

1. Review what you've discovered about your core business interests, your work reward values, and your skills.
2. List and describe the career opportunities at your organization.
3. Draw three concentric circles. That is, draw a large circle on a piece of paper. Within that large circle, draw a somewhat smaller circle. (Make the second circle small enough so that you have room to write between the two circles.) Within that somewhat smaller circle, draw another circle. That central, smallest circle is your career bull's-eye.
4. Identify the opportunities that match your core business interests. In the outermost circle of your career bull's-eye, write down these opportunities. This is your core interests circle.
5. In your core interests circle, underline or highlight those opportunities that also match your most important work reward values.
6. Copy the opportunities you underlined in step 5 into the next inner circle. This is your important values circle.

7. Now underline or highlight those opportunities in your important values circle that also match the skills you now possess or skills you could obtain relatively easily.

8. Copy the opportunities you underlined in step 7 into the centermost circle—your bull's-eye. You've now defined your career target: work that matches your core business interests, your most important work reward values, and your skills.

Steps for Sculpting Your Job

1. Look at the career bull's-eye you created in Steps for Defining Your Career Target.

2. Ask yourself, "Where is the mismatch between my job and the kinds of opportunities that are in my career target?"

3. Divide a piece of paper into three columns. Write "Interests" at the top of the left-hand column, "Values" at the top of the middle column, and "Skills" at the top of the right-hand column. Write down every area you can think of in which your current role does not suit your core business interests, work reward values, and/or skills.

4. Try to think of ways to reshape your current role so that it more closely matches your core interests, values, and skills.

5. Talk with your supervisor about redefining your current role so as to get a better match. When you meet with your supervisor, start by stating the reason you want to brainstorm ways to sculpt your job: "My current role doesn't suit me as well as it

could because _____." (Remember to use the language of core interests, values, and skills.) If possible, be ready to offer solutions and ideas for reshaping your current role so that it's a better match for you and your organization. (Don't just bring a problem; bring a problem and a solution.) Your solutions should include explanations of who will handle any responsibilities you want to let go.

Helping Others Manage Their Careers

EVERY TIME SOMEONE helps someone else—through networking, informational interviewing, and so forth—that person becomes willing to help others in turn. So by helping others, you become part of a constant, informal networking process—a web of people who are willing to provide and receive help.

For example, imagine that one day, Victor, who works in a different department than yours, asks if you know any good engineers he could talk to about making some changes in his career. You do, and you give him a few names. Months later, you might run across Victor and realize that he could help you by recommending, say, some marketing specialists you could talk to about the nature of their work.

Putting your organization first

Just as your colleagues can help you clarify your professional goals and identify growth opportunities in your company, you can do the same for your direct reports or colleagues. In fact, by supporting them in this way, you're doing what's best for your organization.

When you help your direct reports find stimulation and satisfaction in their work, you put your organization first in two ways. First, you encourage talented, ambitious people to stay with the company, so the organization retains valuable employees. You thus support your firm in its efforts to build a stronger workforce. Second, you also help the organization cut costs. After all, finding, hiring, and training replacements are all expensive activities.

Tip: Don't be uncomfortable if a direct report tells you that he or she would like to make some work changes. It doesn't necessarily mean that the person no longer wants to report to you or is deeply unhappy at work, or that he or she is thinking about leaving the company. All it means is that the person is wisely taking charge of his or her career development path.

Speaking the language of interests, values, and skills

To support your direct reports' professional goals, you have to become aware of those goals. An excellent way to become—and stay—aware is to have regular professional development reviews (PDRs) with each of your direct reports.

Try making PDRs part of performance reviews, or conduct them separately. Whichever way you decide to schedule PDRs, make sure you frame the discussion in terms of *core business interests, work reward values,* and *skills.* This focuses the meeting and helps you both talk in specific terms about the person's goals.

Fostering a career management mindset

You can help direct reports adopt a career management mindset and search for opportunities in several ways.

- **Redefine a current role:** Consider redefining a current role so that it better matches the person's interests, values, and skills.

- **Help them network:** Identify individuals in the company who you think could provide growth opportunities, guidance, insight, and even more networking opportunities for your employees. Offer strategies for meeting those individuals, or help to arrange meetings.

- **Evaluate options:** Once you and a direct report have identified possible opportunities, help the person evaluate these opportunities' fit and learning potential. Again, use the language of interests, values, and skills in discussing an opportunity's potential.

Do you supervise managers who have direct reports? If so, you can further reinforce the message that helping others manage their professional development is something your company values. How? Reward managers who excel at this responsibility. Consider evaluating your managers' success in this area as a regular part of performance reviews. And if possible at your organization, tie their compensation to their performance in developing their own direct reports' careers.

Tips and Tools

Tools for Shaping Your Career

Discovery Log

This easy exercise can yield surprisingly insightful results and help you to keep a running list of what you observe or experience about a job or work environment that you like—or don't like. The list items could be about your job or others' and about tasks, relationships, or the environment itself. They could range from "I need to work near a window" to "I can't stand working alone for long periods of time." Since this log is for your eyes only, be blunt and don't censor. After a period of time, review the list to see what themes emerge. Decide what the items tell you about your core business interests and work reward values that can be useful in managing your career.

What I Like	What I Dislike

Skills Assessment

Use this form to develop a baseline assessment of your skills, including those that are transferable from one position to another or those that you want to develop. Rate your current level of proficiency, if desired, from 1 (low, beginning level) to 5 (high, expert level). You may want to supplement this form with skills assessment tools that relate directly to your position, which may be available from your company. You can also use this form to solicit peer feedback on your skill level. Obviously, some of the skills listed below will have no bearing on your career, present or future. Feel free to pass on any such items.

Date of Assessment:

Skill	Level of Proficiency Low 1 2 3 4 5 High					Transferable Yes	No	Key Skill I Want to Develop
Communication Skills								
Writing about Business								
Writing Proposals								
Making Presentations								
Facilitating								
Running Meetings								
Listening								
Interviewing								
Influencing								
Giving and Receiving Feedback								
Resolving Conflicts								
Negotiating								
Writing Creative or Promotional Materials								
Communicating by E-mail								
Editing								
Proofreading								
Writing Job Descriptions								
Other:								
Technology and Computer Skills								
Keyboarding								
Word Processing								
Using Spreadsheets								
Working with HTML								
Working with XML								
Managing Projects								
Using E-mail								
Using Presentation Software								
Using Graphics Software								
Other:								

continued

Skill	Level of Proficiency Low High 1 2 3 4 5					Transferable Yes	No	Key Skill I Want to Develop
Financial Skills								
Budgeting								
Analyzing Financial Information								
Cost Accounting								
Forecasting								
Tracking and Managing								
Preparing a Business Plan								
Preparing an Investment Initiative								
Analyzing Cash Flow								
Determining Breakeven Point								
Using Quantitative Analysis								
Other:								
Supervisory Skills								
Hiring								
Coaching								
Delegating								
Setting Goals and Objectives								
Directing								
Assessing Performance								
Leading								
Motivating								
Training								
Analyzing Work Flow and Processes								
Recruiting and Retaining Employees								
Managing Administrative Tasks								
Other:								
Management Skills								
Leading Change								
Managing Customers, Internal and/or External								
Orchestrating Projects								
Managing Production or Implementation								
Managing Your Boss								
Solving Business Problems								
Thinking Critically about Business Issues								
Consulting and Networking								
Managing Vendors								
Planning Strategy								
Planning Tactics								
Thinking Creatively, Brainstorming								
Managing for Innovation								
Managing a Diverse Workforce								
Marketing for International Sales								
Teamwork Skills								
Leading a Team								
Engaging in Group Problem Solving								

Skill	Level of Proficiency Low → High 1 2 3 4 5		Transferable Yes	No	Key Skill I Want to Develop
Teamwork Skills, *continued*					
Keeping Teams on Target					
Working with a Virtual Team					
Assuming Team Membership Roles					
Collaborating					
Other:					
Self-Management Skills					
Knowing Yourself					
Cultivating Emotional Intelligence					
Managing Your Time					
Balancing Work and Life					
Developing Your Career					
Handling Stress					
Setting Limits and Goals					
Using Power and Authority Positively					
Seeing Multiple Perspectives					
Other:					
Sales and Marketing Skills					
Marketing Products or Services					
Engaging in Direct Marketing					
Performing or Directing Market Research					
Telemarketing					
Developing Promotions					
Handling Publicity					
Using Electronic Marketing					
Managing Trade Shows/Exhibits					
Marketing to Consumers					
Marketing to Businesses					
Analyzing the Competition					
Engaging in Direct Sales					
Forecasting Sales					
Engaging in Telesales					
Engaging Consultative Selling					
Other:					
Physical and Manual Dexterity Skills					
Assembling, Constructing, or Building					
Operating Tools or Machinery					
Fixing or Repairing					
Training Others on Tasks					
Other Industry and/or Job-Specific Skills (List)					

Informational Interviewing

Use this form to help you prepare for an informational interview.

Discussion with: **Date:**

Objectives

What do you really want to get out of this interview? What would make it successful for you?

Marketplace

What are your projections for this type of work or industry? Is it stable, growing, declining?

What are the key trends or issues? New developments? Key challenges?

What and where are the opportunities?

What are typical salaries in this type of job, entry-level to experienced? What are the opportunities for career growth?

Entry into Position

When and how did you get involved in this work?

What was your training and background? Is this typical for people in your position and in similar positions?

How important are specific credentials for entry or success?

Job Specifics

What's a typical day like for you or someone in a similar position?

What do you like most about your work?

What do you like least?

What talents or skills do you think are the most crucial to success in this work?

What attitudes or values are important?

Who doesn't do well in this type of work?

How do you advance or get promoted in this type of work?

Recommendations

Would my background be appropriate for this type of work?

What would you recommend I do if I want to go into this type of work?

Are there other jobs similar to yours that you would suggest I also consider?

Can you recommend other people I can talk to, or other resources I can check out?

Knowing what you do now, would you approach this career (or job) in the same way? If not, what would you do differently, and why?

Rewards

Use this worksheet to think through what really motivates you at work. You can also rate each item from low (1) priority or value to high (5). Review these ratings as you assess your degree of satisfaction with your current job, or use them as a guide to what you'd be looking for in your next position. If you are a supervisor, you may use this as part of a development discussion with a direct report.

	Level of Importance or Value Low 1 2 3 4 High 5
Financial Gain This position provides an excellent opportunity for financial reward.	
Power and Influence The position offers the opportunity to exercise power and influence and the chance to be an influential decision maker.	
Lifestyle The position fits with my desired lifestyle. It lets me balance work and life demands and interests.	
Autonomy The position offers me autonomy and independence—the ability to work without a lot of close supervision.	
Affiliation The position lets me work with colleagues I enjoy and admire and gives me a sense of belonging to a group.	
Workspace The location and physical workspace are desirable and offer me benefits such as a pleasing environment, an easy commute, or accessibility to day care.	
Intellectual Stimulation The position is interesting and challenging and offers learning and development opportunities.	
Competence This position offers me the opportunity to build competence or expertise in an area.	
Recognition and Support In this position and work environment, my contributions are recognized and valued. My development is supported as well.	

Other

List additional specific rewards that you value.

Assessment

Reviewing your ratings above, what jumps out at you as most important? Least important? How well does your current job meet your reward needs?

Are there some actions you can take so that your work better satisfies your needs, such as modifying your work, taking on a "stretch" assignment, or spending more time with colleagues you enjoy?

Career Self-Assessment

Use the following questions to help you think through your developmental needs and goals. Supplement this form with others such as the Rewards Worksheet to pull together a plan for your next developmental step.

Current and Future Work Situation

What's the overall fit between your current position and your interests, values, and skills?

What is your overall level of satisfaction with your current position? Are you beginning to sense it's time for a change?

Do you anticipate that any of the following changes will occur in the foreseeable future? (Check all that apply.)

- ☐ Change in supervisor
- ☐ Relocation: another part of country or international
- ☐ Corporate downsizing or merger
- ☐ Change in the type of work you do
- ☐ Transfer to another division or part of the company
- ☐ Change to supervisory role

- ☐ Change in job
- ☐ Change in workspace
- ☐ Change in employer
- ☐ Promotion
- ☐ Job redefined or enlarged

What are the implications of any anticipated changes? Will you need to learn new skills? Will a change result in a more or less favorable position for you in terms of job fit and opportunity?

Skills: Strengths and Gaps

What are your top five skills (i.e., those where you have the most proficiency and/or those you enjoy using the most)?

What are the top two or three skills you need to learn in order to grow in your job, advance to the next level, or seek a new job?

What are your key transferable skills—those skills that are not just job-specific but that can be applied to work in many positions? Example: basic computer skills, negotiation skills, financial analysis.

continued

What do you think others would say are your strengths?

The Next Step and Opportunity

As a next step towards your long-term career goals, where do you see yourself six to twelve months from now?

What are some developmental opportunities you can take advantage of?

What parts of your work would you like to continue doing or do with more skill?

What new work activities or positions would you like to try?

What are your short-term career development goals?

What support do you need to achieve them? (Training, people, time, money, etc.)

What do you think others would say about your work and your career aspirations and plans?

Test Yourself

This section offers ten multiple-choice questions to help you identify your baseline knowledge of career management. Answers to
the questions are given at the end of the test.

1. What three self-knowledge areas are the most important in
defining and navigating your career path?

   a. Your five-year goals, family values, and financial needs.

   b. Your core business interests, work values, and skills.

   c. Your short- and long-term goals, core business interests, and
      skills.

2. What are the three main information sources for knowing
yourself?

   a. Yourself, others (colleagues, friends, and family), and assess-
      ment tools.

   b. Your boss, your nighttime dreams, and a group-therapy
      program.

   c. Your family, your friends, and your career counselor.

3. Who is *most* responsible for management of your career?

    a. Your supervisor.

    b. Your company overall (including its career resources department, if it has one).

    c. You.

4. Of your core business interests, work values, and skills, which one area is the most important in identifying appropriate growth opportunities at work?

    a. Core business interests.

    b. Work values.

    c. Skills.

5. Which of the following is the most important benefit of taking charge of your own career?

    a. You're guaranteed to earn more money and get promoted.

    b. Your company doesn't have to invest in a career center.

    c. You find more satisfaction in your work and become a more valuable employee for your company.

6. Which of the following are examples of the eight core business functions that let you express your deepest work interests?

    a. Enterprise Control, Influence through Language and Ideas, and Using Your Intuition.

    b. Application of Technology, Counseling and Mentoring, and Enterprise Control.

    c. Understanding Spreadsheets, Giving Inspiring Speeches, and Managing Work/Life Balance.

7. Decide whether the following statement is true or false: To better match your work with your core business interests, values, and skills, you can collaborate with your supervisor to redefine your current role.

   a. True.
   b. False.

8. Which of the following metaphors best captures the nature of career development today as opposed to earlier times?

   a. A lattice versus a ladder.
   b. A bicycle versus a pogo stick.
   c. A moored rowboat versus a ship tossing on the ocean.

9. The best developmental opportunities in your organization:

   a. Perfectly match your interests, values, and skills.
   b. Stretch you by offering challenges that encourage you to learn new skills and knowledge.
   c. Encourage you to try work that you know nothing about.

10. Decide whether the following statement is true or false: To obtain the skills you need to perform in a new position, you must go back to school and earn a degree.

   a. True.
   b. False.

Answers to test questions

1, b. These three self-knowledge areas together form the basis for guiding and managing your career. By understanding what business activities interest you, what workplace rewards you value most, and what you do best, you can define your professional goals.

2, a. By getting to know your core business interests, work reward values, and skills through self-reflection exercises; by collecting feedback from colleagues, friends, and family; and by using any of the available assessment tools, you compile a powerful body of knowledge that will let you define and pursue the best career opportunities for you.

3, c. The business world has experienced enormous, rapidly accelerating changes. The traditional unspoken contract between employer and employee—in which companies took responsibility for employees' career paths—no longer exists at many companies. Therefore, each of us is responsible for managing our own professional development.

4, a. If you're not passionately interested in your work, you'll soon get bored or burn out—no matter how good you are at your job or how much it offers the rewards you value the most.

5, c. When you manage your own career, you help yourself derive more satisfaction from your work. When you're more satisfied at work, you perform better and feel more committed to your job and organization—which also helps your company.

6, b. All three of these are examples of core business interests. The eight core business interests are (1) Application of Technology, (2) Quantitative Analysis, (3) Theory Development and Conceptual Thinking, (4) Creative Production, (5) Counseling and Mentoring, (6) Managing People and Relationships, (7) Enterprise Control, and (8) Influence through Language and Ideas.

7, a. Always assume that you can redefine your current role to better suit you. If you're a high performer, your supervisor will likely be glad to support your efforts in this area. After all, he or she will get to keep you rather than lose you to another position in the company.

8, a. A lattice conveys the idea that professional development opportunities now exist at all levels and in all departments within most organizations. You can move freely among them depending on which opportunities best suit you and your organization.

9, b. You want development opportunities to help you hone new skills and acquire new knowledge—that's what makes work more satisfying to you, and you more valuable to your company. But don't pick an assignment that stretches you too much. A good rule of thumb is that if you think it will take more than six months to deliver excellent performance in the new role, the assignment probably will be *too* much of a stretch.

10, b. There are many other ways to gain new skills besides going back to school. These include volunteering, reading magazines, sharing jobs, and so forth—steps that don't require the time and expense of getting a new degree.

Frequently Asked Questions

Are core business interests determined when you're young, and do they remain unchanged throughout your life?

They're generally determined by your early twenties. By that time, there's a discernible pattern, and the basic contours of that pattern remain remarkably stable.

How were the eight core business interests developed?

They were developed from analysis of thousands of people's responses on tests about their interests at work. The core interests describe fundamental, essential activities of business work.

What's the most common mistake people make in thinking about their careers?

The most common mistake is basing career decisions on what you think you *should* do or what you *can* do—not on what most interests or moves you. You probably have lots of abilities that you're not interested in applying as a regular part of your work. This is an easy trap to fall into. Another trap, especially for people whose careers are just beginning, is going for the job that pays the most. We each should think at least as much about *learning* as about *earning*.

What are some easy ways for people to identify their core business interests?

You can perform active-imagination exercises, in which you reflect on what kinds of work have most inspired you or captured your attention in the past. You can also flip through six months' worth of issues of *Business Week* or *Fortune* and pay attention to what kinds of articles, advertisements, and so on most draw your attention. Look especially for the difference between feeling that you have to *turn* your attention to a particular topic versus feeling that a topic *pulls* your attention.

Can a person have more than one core business interest?

Yes. Often a person will have two or three main interests, with perhaps one of them most dominant.

How have attitudes toward work and career changed?

There's been a change in the idea of what a job is. Many people don't even use the word *job* anymore; instead, they use *work opportunity*. More and more, there aren't jobs per se, as in, "Here's your job, your title, and your desk, and you'll probably be here for five years." Now you're more likely to hear, "We've got a problem or a project, you've got a skill set and a background that can help us. When it's done, we'll have a conversation, and maybe there will be other problems you can help us with. And maybe there won't." The duration of the work opportunity is therefore the *project* duration.

This is true not just for freelancers but also for full-time employees. You may remain an employee for a long time, but your responsibilities may change regularly. This is also true for employees of *any* age—not just 25-year-olds.

What proportion of people find satisfying work?

It's an ongoing search for everyone these days. People do find it, but we all have to keep refining our concept of it and moving toward it. Even though our core business interests remain stable over time, the opportunities to express them depend on economic and other situations that are constantly changing. So, you've got to frequently reengage with the change process.

How can people broach the subject of career change with their immediate supervisors if their supervisors don't want to lose them?

The best way is to frame the discussion in terms of job sculpting: how you can redefine your current role so that it better matches your core business interests, work reward values, and skills. Also, come prepared with solutions for handling the ramifications of any change. For example, if you want to let go of certain responsibilities, how do you suggest they would be handled? If there's simply no opportunity to redefine your role, explore other opportunities within the company. In firms that emphasize retention, your supervisor will be rewarded for helping good employees find new opportunities inside the company.

If I contact people to request an informational interview or a networking discussion, won't they think that I'm just trying to use them?

No—not if you're sincere and you respect their time. Be sure to show them that you appreciate the information they're sharing. Remember: You're not so much asking for a job as you're asking for information. Most people enjoy talking about their work. Explain that someone else whom the person knows and respects recommended him or her as an excellent person for you to talk with, and ask for just twenty minutes of the person's time.

It seems that required skills are always changing. How can I get the skills I need to keep moving forward in my career?

Many people automatically assume that they have to go back to school to get a degree in order to acquire new skills. That's absolutely not true. Continuing education classes are one less time-consuming and less expensive alternative. But there are lots of other ways to learn, too—such as job shadowing, stretch assignments at work, seminars, video- or audiotapes, books, newsletters, online or distance learning, volunteering opportunities, and so on. The key is to assess your options and pick the best ones for your learning style and your skill needs as well as for your budget and schedule.

Everyone's so busy at my company that no one seems to know what's going on in departments other than their own. How can I find out about work opportunities under these conditions?

You can start talking with people from other departments to find out what kinds of work they do, what the culture is like in those departments, and so forth. Also, try asking to be invited to meetings that you normally might not think of attending. Take advantage of all the companywide events and learning opportunities that your firm offers. That's a great way to simply start getting to know people and learning more about how the company operates. From there, you can begin identifying opportunities and drawing on the network of people you've established for information.

Will my work reward values change much over the years?

They will probably change somewhat, depending on the different phases of life you go through. For example, if you're starting a family, financial security and opportunities for long-term saving might become your top reward value. If you're just starting out in the work world, opportunities to travel might be your most important value.

To Learn More

Articles

Butler, Timothy, and James Waldroop. "Job Sculpting: The Art of Retaining Your Best People." *Harvard Business Review* (February 2000).

Helping people define their ideal jobs benefits everyone: employees, their managers, and the organization. This article shows how managers can play a central role in this process, retaining valuable employees by customizing work to better match employees' deepest interests.

Butler, Timothy, and James Waldroop. "Understanding 'People People.'" *Harvard Business Review* (June 2004).

Because people do their best work when it most closely matches their interests, the authors contend, managers can increase productivity by taking into account employees' relational interests and skills when making personnel choices and project assignments. After analyzing the psychological tests of more than 7,000 business professionals, the authors identified four dimensions of relational work: influence, interpersonal facilitation, relational creativity, and team leadership. Understanding these four dimensions will help you get optimal performance from your employees, appropriately reward their work, and assist them in setting career goals. It will also help you make better choices when it comes to your own career development. To get started, try the authors' free online assessment tool, which measures both your orientation toward relational work in general and your interest level in each of its four dimensions.

Gary, Loren. "The Next Ideas: Rethinking Money and Motivation." *Harvard Management Update* (April 2004).

Because our attitudes toward money reveal so much about our personalities, perhaps concerns about money can reveal our deep-seated interests. Ever heard the advice, "Do what you love and the money will follow"? For the last half-century, it's been the prevailing view among management thinkers. But now, social critics and executive coaches alike are struck by the way in which an increasingly affluent culture can make the search for meaning and purpose more difficult and are showing a keen interest in the psychology of money.

Nash, Laura, and Howard Stevenson. "Success That Lasts." *Harvard Business Review* (April 2004).

Nash and Stevenson have built a practical framework for a new way of thinking about success—a way that leads to personal and professional fulfillment instead of feelings of anxiety and stress. The authors' research uncovered four irreducible components of success: happiness (feelings of pleasure or contentment about your life); achievement (accomplishments that compare favorably against similar goals others have strived for); significance (the sense that you've made a positive impact on people you care about); and legacy (a way to establish your values or accomplishments so as to help others find future success). People who achieve lasting success, the authors learned, tend to rely on a kaleidoscope strategy to structure their aspirations and activities. This article explains how to build your own kaleidoscope framework.

Books

Boldt, Laurence G. *Zen and the Art of Making a Living: A Practical Guide to Creative Career Design*. New York: Penguin/Arkana, 1999.

In the author's view, everyone is the "artist" of his or her own life. Part I helps you identify deeply satisfying work. Part II provides practical steps to finding or creating that work. A wealth of worksheets, ideas, and strategies supplement the author's ideas.

Butler, Timothy. *Getting Unstuck: How Dead Ends Become New Paths*. Boston: Harvard Business School Press, 2007.

The author provides strategies for moving beyond a career impasse—by recognizing the state of impasse, awakening your imagination, recognizing patterns of meaning in your life, and taking action for change. Drawing on a wealth of stories about individuals who have successfully transitioned out of impasses, this book gives you a practical, authoritative road map for moving past your immediate impasse—and defining a meaningful path forward.

Butler, Timothy, and James Waldroop. *Discovering Your Career in Business*. Cambridge, MA: Perseus Books, 1997.

This book presents the theoretical framework behind the Harvard ManageMentor PLUS "Managing Your Career" topic and the authors' Internet-based career self-assessment and management program, CareerLeader. The authors provide valuable case examples and exercises for identifying your core business interests.

Butler, Timothy, and James Waldroop. *Maximum Success: Changing the Twelve Behavior Patterns That Keep You from Getting Ahead*. New York: Currency/Doubleday, 2000.

Part of managing your own career development is knowing which behaviors are keeping you from your full potential. Using nearly forty years of field research, the authors describe the twelve most common problem-behavior patterns, explore the psychological reasons behind them, and show you how to change them for maximum performance.

Wademan, Daisy. *Remember Who You Are: Life Stories That Inspire the Heart and Mind*. Boston: Harvard Business School Press, 2004.

Leadership requires many attributes besides intelligence and business savvy—courage, character, compassion, and respect are just a few. New managers learn concrete skills in the classroom or on the job, but where do they hone the equally important human values that will guide them through a career that is both successful and meaningful? In this inspirational book, the author gathers lessons on balancing the personal and professional responsibilities of leadership from faculty members of Harvard Business School. Offering a rare glimpse inside the classrooms in which many of the world's prominent leaders are trained, *Remember Who You Are* imparts lessons learned not in business but in life.

Sources for
Shaping Your Career

We would like to acknowledge the sources who aided in developing this topic.

Billington, Jim. "Meet Your New Mentor: It's a Network." *Harvard Management Update* (August 1997).

Boldt, Laurence G. *Zen and the Art of Making a Living: A Practical Guide to Creative Career Design.* New York: Penguin/Arkana, 1999.

Bolles, Richard N. *The Three Boxes of Life and How to Get Out of Them.* Berkeley, CA: Ten Speed Press, 1981.

Butler, Timothy, and James Waldroop. *Discovering Your Career in Business.* Cambridge, MA: Perseus Books, 1997.

———. "Job Sculpting: The Art of Retaining Your Best People." *Harvard Business Review* (September–October 1999).

Carlone, Katie. Personal communication. September 13, 2000.

Farren, Caela. *Who's Running Your Career?* Austin, TX: Bard Press, 1997.

Hakim, Cliff. *We Are All Self-Employed.* San Francisco: Berrett-Koehler, 1994.

Hill, Linda. "Managing Your Career." Harvard Business School Note, December 15, 1998. Product no. 9-494-082.

Koonce, Richard. "How to Prevent Professional Obsolescence." *Training & Development* (February 1999).

McCall, Jr., Morgan W. *High Flyers: Developing the Next Generation of Leaders.* Boston: Harvard Business School Press, 1998.

Moscs, Barbara. *The Good News about Careers: How You'll Be Working in the Next Decade.* San Francisco: Jossey-Bass, 1999.

Waterman, Jr., Robert H., Judith A. Waterman, and Betsy A. Collard. "Toward a Career-Resilient Workforce." *Harvard Business Review* (July–August 1994).

Notes

Notes

Notes

Notes

Notes

Notes

Notes

Notes

Notes

Notes

Notes

Notes

Notes

How to Order

Harvard Business Press publications are available worldwide from your local bookseller or online retailer.

You can also call:
1-800-668-6780

Our product consultants are available to help you 8:00 a.m.– 6:00 p.m., Monday–Friday, Eastern Time. Outside the U.S. and Canada, call: 617-783-7450.

Please call about special discounts for quantities greater than ten.

You can order online at:
www.HBSPress.org